Extensive banking experience in one of Africa's foremost financial institutions, coupled with high educational and professional training are her selling points. Professionally, she has managed key areas of the banking business, managed and coordinated activities at the executive level, which have given her insights into practical business management.

She has attended career enhancing training programmes such as Citibank Global Markets Clients' Training and Bourse Game, Strategic Assets and Liabilities Management (BTRM), Treasury Risk Management; Risk Management in Banks and the Capital Implications (Fitch Learning), Assets and Liabilities Management (INSEAD), Supervisory Skills, International Trade Finance (CITIBANK).

She has the internationally recognised professional postgraduate diploma in governance, risk and compliance from the International Compliance Association and Alliance Manchester Business School; as well as a treasury dealing certificate from the Financial Markets' Association (ACI).

With a Doctorate in Business Administration and a double MBA in International Business; and Banking and Finance, Patricia is a highly skilled business professional with extensive professional and academic qualification for managing businesses.

The author is currently a business lecturer in one of the UK's universities where she helps train the next generation of business leaders.

To my family

Patricia Barnett-Quaicoo

BUSINESS MANAGEMENT SOLUTIONS

Practical Steps for Solving Problems in Your Business

AUSTIN MACAULEY PUBLISHERS™

LONDON • CAMBRIDGE • NEW YORK • SHARJAH

A CIP catalogue record for this title is available from the British Library.

ISBN 9781398495104 (Paperback)
ISBN 9781398495111 (ePub e-book)

www.austinmacauley.co.uk

First Published 2024
Austin Macauley Publishers Ltd®
1 Canada Square
Canary Wharf
London
E14 5AA

This publication has been made possible through the contribution of everyone who has supported my academic and professional pursuits.

Table of Contents

Chapter One
Introduction

I have gone through the rudiments of practical corporate experience as well as academic preparation in my quest to become a seasoned business professional.

For 16 years I worked in a bank in Ghana and had the opportunity of working with various units as I climbed the corporate ladder. At various stages, I came across once vibrant businesses beginning to struggle and unable to meet their financial obligations. Though a few of the reasons for the struggling companies were external factors beyond the control of the management of these businesses, many of these dwindling business cases were as a result of wrong management decisions.

You would wonder why the owner of a financial institution would influence the decision of loan acquisition to benefit his friends and not expect to have high incidences of non-performing loans? Again, why would the board and management of a manufacturing company refuse to innovate by embracing technological advancement to stay in the competition simply because they think it is better to stick to the old trusted ways no matter how inefficient?

…And just in case you were beginning to think these problems were peculiar to Ghana or Africa, then hold your horses! My observation of the business of business management transcends African boundaries.

Enrolling in a doctorate in business administration programme in the United Kingdom required as part of my academic study, to identify problems with companies…and oh did I find many with problems! Indeed it was such a surprise to realise that some of the big names had issues with the management of their human resources, while others could simply not go through a transformation of their organisations even though it was evident that was the best thing to do. There were others suffering a crisis of leadership that affected the planning and implementation of an effective strategy for the advancement of the business.

I also had a working stint as a research analyst with an investment company that specialised in acquisition of SMEs. Here again most of the problems I had encountered were present on a smaller scale.

Then, during the masterclasses of the ICA professional postgraduate diploma in governance, risk and compliance, I had the rare opportunity of meeting global business leaders from different countries. As they shared their stories, I realised that problems such as effective governance, risk and compliance was such an important ingredient in business management.

After these experiences, I realised that irrespective of geographical location or size, the issues confronting business managers were quite common and range from the inability to create or maintain value, to lack of leadership and strategic thinking.

I have therefore compiled some of the most critical observations essential for successful business management to help as a guide for business owners, managers and business students. This book is not meant to be a panacea for all the problems but as a guide in order to seek for the appropriate help.

Chapter Two
Create Value

Wealth is created from creating value.
– Randy Gage

Value creation is the foundation and purpose of a business. Businesses must create value to produce the needed financial returns and stay competitive. If businesses fail to create value, they collapse!

Value creation is a qualitative approach to improving value through the improvement of strategy and business modules. It involves a careful exploration of existing strategy and the change of strategy and business module, where necessary, towards the improvement of the value of the business for the development of a sustainable competitive advantage. Simply, value creation is the generation of revenue which exceeds the expenses, resulting in value or profit to the stakeholder. It can also be broadened to include increase in sales and the creation of brand value and equity. It is the basis for the existence of the company and is beneficial in achieving increased product sales, increase in price, and insuring the future availability of funding.

According to Gautam Mahajan, in the past, value creation was intended for the benefit of shareholders and investors of a company. However, today, the concept has metamorphosed to benefit all stakeholders such as partners, employees, customers, society, labour unions and inherently investors and shareholders (Mahajan, 2016).

The Concept of Value and Value Creation

Mahajan's five laws of value creation state that:

i. Value creation is a basic requirement or a necessity for the advancement of human activity, progress and creativity.
ii. Value creation is proactively exceeding what is basically expected of you or your job.
iii. Value creation impacts all stakeholders.
iv. Value creation leverages a person's or an organisation's potential, learning, and creativity while making it meaningful and worthwhile for people to belong and perform both physically and emotionally (Mahajan, 2016).

Businesses can therefore create value only when the concept of value and value creation are fully understood. Philosophers, economists, management scientists and engineers have attempted to define the concept of value in various ways: ethicists and philosophers study the values held by individuals and societies to govern good behaviour whilst management scientists research into the significance of values and the contribution it makes to a business.

The numerous definitions of value by economists and scholars include Alfred Marshall's where value is defined as 'the equilibrium price when marginal cost is equals marginal utility' (Frisch, 1950) and Michael Porter's which states that 'value is what buyers are willing to pay for a good or service' (Porter, 1985).

However, Baier's definition of value as 'the capacity of a good, service or activity for the satisfaction of a need or the provision of a benefit to an individual or a legal entity', is more appropriate for this discussion.

The concept of value creation involves the following:

- Value Addition and value erosion.
- Value, cost, margin and profit.
- Resource combinations for new value creation.
- Financial value addition.
- Shareholder value creation, dynamics and management.

Value Creation Process

The value creation process involves a strategic analysis of the organisation's current state and taking actions based on the results of the analysis to ensure future sustainability. Strategic analysis of a company requires an internal and external analysis, a horizontal and vertical analysis of financial statements and a value chain analysis. The strategic analysis leads to an identification of the organisation's business model, strategy, competitive advantage, value-based inadequacies.

Internal and External Analysis

Internal analysis reviews an organisation's resources through the perusal of organisational activities and linking them with the organisation for the identification of its strengths and capabilities. This equips the firm with the knowledge of competencies and necessary improvement for the selection of the opportunities to be tapped in line with its capacity by focusing on factors within its domain. The firm is also able to assess its capacity-gap and take steps by matching its objectives to its capacity for a selection of areas of growth in consonance with its potential. External analysis examines the things outside a company such as competition, new opportunities and economic conditions, which can affect its success while internal analysis identifies and evaluates a company's specific characteristics including competencies, capabilities and resources. This analysis can be performed using analytical models such as value chain analysis, 5-forces and PESTEL, the results of which are fed into the SWOT analysis of a company.

External analysis involves an assessment of the wider business environment for an understanding of the environment in which a business operates. When a business appreciates its environment, it discerns the threats and opportunities prevalent in that business sector and is able to plan strategically for the success of the business.

Value Chain Analysis

Value chain analysis is a strategic mechanism for the identification of a company's primary and support activities by determining which of a firm's activities are most valuable and must be performed by the firm itself and those activities which can be outsourced to be performed by others. Michael Porter suggested that the activities of a company can be put into two groups of primary and support activities. Primary activities are those linked directly to the creation of a product and include inbound logistics, operations, outbound logistics, marketing and sales whiles support activities are those not directly linked to production, but which can increase efficiency.

Value chain analysis helps in the identification of the activities that can lead to a competitive advantage of the company, but the vision and strategy of a company can be lost as the operations are split into segments because the value chain does not link the various components together.

Some models of analyses that can be used for the internal and external analysis of businesses in relation to value creation include Porter's 5-Forces analysis and PESTEL analysis.

External Analysis

Porter's 5-Forces Analysis

Michael Porter's 5-forces model of analysis was developed to analyse the competitive environment a product or company exists in. It is used for the analysis of the business environment in which an organisation operates and helps in understanding the industry and its participants. It also helps to evaluate how changes in the business' environment affect the profitability of an organisation. These five forces are the threat of new entrants, the threat of suppliers, the threat of buyers, the threat of substitute products, and the threat of competitive rivalry. The 5-forces model is beneficial in identifying and analysing five competitive forces which outline every company and help to determine the company's weaknesses and strengths (Porter, 2008).

1. Threat of New Entrants

The power of a company can be affected by the ease at which new entrants can enter into that market or industry. Generally, it is easier for competitors to enter a sector which does not require a huge initial capital and has fewer industry restrictions. It is easier for competitors to enter a market if it does not require a huge initial capital.

2. Threat of Suppliers

It can be possible for suppliers to drive up the price of goods and services if the number of suppliers of key goods or services is small. The fewer the number of suppliers, the more dependent a company is on a supplier and the more power a supplier wields.

3. Threat of Buyers

This threat addresses the ability of buyers to drive prices down. It is affected by how many buyers a firm has, and the purchasing power of these buyers and how much it cost buyers to from moving from one company to the other. Buyers are more powerful if they are few.

4. Threat of Substitutes

Substitute goods or services from competitors which can be used to replace a company's products or services pose a threat. Products or services that can easily be substituted weaken the power of a company.

5. Competitive Rivalry

This force is important in determining the number of competitors a company has and the threat they pose to the company.

PESTEL Analysis

PESTEL is an acronym for the political, economic, social, technological, environmental and legal factors which affect companies. PESTEL analysis is a tool employed for the analysis and monitoring of the macro-environmental (external environment) factors which have a bearing on a firm.

Internal Analysis

Horizontal and Vertical Comparative Analysis of Financial Statements

Vertical analysis which is also called *common-size analysis analyses* financial statements by presenting every item on the statement as a percentage of a chosen base figure from the statement. In a *vertical analysis of the* balance sheet, usually, total assets are used as the base figure for the items under assets and the total liabilities and stockholders' equity is used as the base figure for the liabilities. Individual assets and liabilities are then shown as percentages of the respective base figures.

Horizontal analysis or trend analysis is a method for analysing financial statements by showing variations in the amounts of corresponding financial statement items over a specified interval. To conduct a horizontal analysis, at least two financial statements (e.g. balance sheet or income statement) of the same type for different periods for the same company are compared, using the earlier dated statement as the base. The results of this comparative analysis can either be expressed in absolute values or percentages (Ferrel, 2012). This helps a business to identify which aspects of its internal environment to focus on for value creation.

Application

A multinational oil and gas company with its headquarters in London and affiliated to several other organisations faces stiff competition from other operators in the competitive global oil and gas industry coupled with unimpressive financial performance. The company's brand has suffered negative brand equity due to the current unimpressive performance.

The company therefore needs to ensure that value is created to avoid its collapse.

Applying what has been discussed earlier, the current situation of the company needs to analysed to identify areas of the business which can be earmarked for value creation.

Current Business Model

As an oil and gas company, its operations are divided into three—upstream, midstream and downstream. In the upstream are all activities in oil and natural gas exploration, development of oil fields and production, supply base renewal, exploration and evaluation, safety, reliability and compliance of drilling operations. Operations in the midstream activities link upstream and downstream. These include the processing of natural gas and transportation of crude oil from the oil well to refineries and other users carry out these activities. The transportation is done using large transportation mechanisms such as tankers and pipes.

The downstream of has international manufacturing and marketing operations made up of three businesses namely fuels, lubricants and petrochemicals.

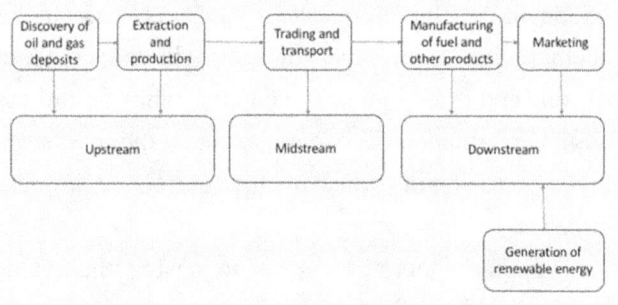

5-Forces Analysis

The different levels of threat posed by the five components were identified. The threat posed by new entrants was insignificant with the huge entry capital requirement serving as a deterrent. It was identified that the low bargaining powers of buyers was low due to the difficulty of switching costs and the determination of prices on a global level. Though the substitute products posed a low threat, this situation was likely to change as governments continue to embrace policies to protect the planet by discouraging the use of fossil fuels. The suppliers' threat is medium but there is a keen competition between large industry players.

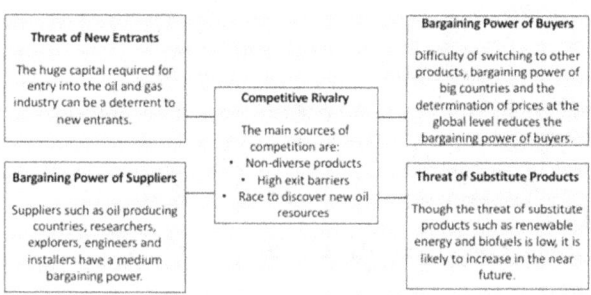

Threat of New Entrants

The threat of new entrants into the petroleum industry could adversely affect the profitability of the company, however, despite the attractiveness of the industry, this threat is very low due to the high initial investments associated with the operations of this industry.

Bargaining Power of Buyers

In the petroleum sector, the price of crude oil is fixed globally and relies on the economic relationship within global demand and supply, but some degree of power can be applied by countries with high consumption, such as the United States of America, Japan or China. The homogenous nature of the product and the difficulty of substituting costs are making the bargaining power of buyers medium.

Threats of Substitute Products

Substitute commodities affect the pricing of products and limit the profitability of an industry. In the oil industry, substitutes include biofuels and renewable resources. The risk from these alternative sources is quite minimal because they are still in a developmental process. However, globally governments are embracing polices for the protection of the planet by discouraging the use of fossil fuels, signifying a low threat for the oil industry.

Bargaining Power of Suppliers

Suppliers can impact its operations by increasing prices or decreasing the quality of products or services because the company is surrounded by an intricate chain of suppliers, including suppliers of oil fields and expertise. The nature of this complex number of suppliers provides the company with a choice from a wide range of dealers, thereby making the bargaining power of suppliers medium.

Industry Competitors

The petroleum industry is characterised by the presence of few major competitors and many others with less influence. The strongest companies are those with developed expertise. The risk of drying oil wells has generated keen competition among big companies to merge with or acquire smaller companies.

PESTEL Analysis

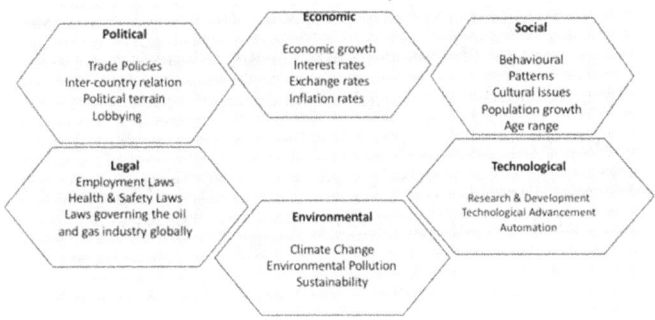

Political Factors

Governmental policies such as political terrain, trading policies, inter-countries relations, and lobbying affect the operations of the company. Primarily, these factors affect the location and timing of extraction. Political instabilities therefore drive volatilities in the global petroleum market. Also, the governments are becoming more aware of the negative effects of climate caused by carbon dioxide emissions; many have adopted renewable forms of energy by adhering to the United Nations' Paris Climate Change Agreement (United Nations, 2016).

Economic Factors

Economic factors affecting the operations of the company include economic growth, interest rates, exchange rates and inflation rates. The petroleum industry has a significant connection with the global economy therefore global economic growth impacts directly on the consumption of petroleum products. Any adverse effect on the global economy is therefore of major concern to the company.

Social Factors

Social factors impacting the company may include behavioural patterns of the inhabitants of the location of oil wells, average age of society and the rate of population growth. Hostility of the local inhabitants towards staff of the oil company can adversely affect production. The average age of the population is also important as a healthy and available workforce is an incentive for the operations of the company.

Technological Factors

Another external factor is technology since technology is used throughout its value chain to operate efficiently, with the increasing demand for technological advancement posing a great challenge.

Environmental Factors

Some recent oil spillages have negatively affected the oil and gas company. Measures put in place company to ensure no recurrence include the protection of freshwater bodies, aqua quality and biodiversity.

Legal Factors

The company has been faced with many legal and ethical issues concerning safety violations, ethically questionable and illegal behaviour, which have impacted negatively on the company's brand equity and value.

Summary of PESTEL Analysis

Generally, the company has handled its external issues well but continues to be plagued by some of the environmental issues caused by the recent oil spillage and its related legal issues.

SWOT Analysis

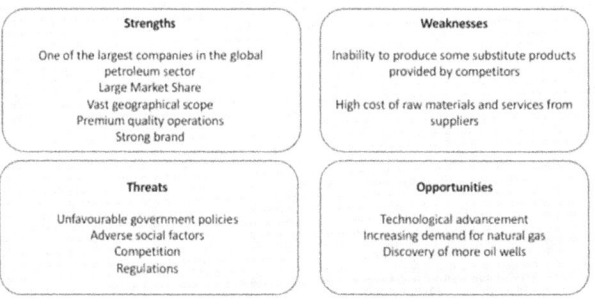

SWOT Analysis is a simple tool for analysing the Strengths and Weaknesses, and the Opportunities and Threats that an organisation faces. The results of obtained from the 5-forces and the PESTEL analysis feed into the SWOT Analysis. The strengths and weaknesses of the company as identified through the 5-forces analysis were as follows:

Strengths

- One of the biggest companies in the petroleum sector.
- Large market share.
- Vast geographical scope.
- Premium quality operations.
- Very strong brand.

Weaknesses

- Competitive rivalry.
- Substitute products.
- Bargaining power of suppliers.

The opportunities and threats identified from the PESTEL were as follows:

Opportunities

- Technological advancement.
- Increasing natural gas market.
- More oil well discoveries.
- Expand export market.
- Investment in alternate business.

Threats

- Unfavourable government policies.
- Global economic crises.
- Adverse social factors.
- High competition.
- Environment regulations.
- Lawsuits concerning the company's ecological activities.

Existing Competitive Advantage

The oil company derives its competitive advantage from its strengths and the opportunities available to the company. The enviable position of being one of the biggest companies in the petroleum sector with a large market share and a vast geographical scope positions strategically over its competitors. A strong brand which forms the basis of their business, underpinning the premium quality operations of the company and serving as a guide for customers with the help of their logo ensures the sustenance of the company's position in the industry. The application of technological advancement leads to the discovery of oil deposits and greatly increases the production capacity of the company and advancement in renewable energy.

Existing Strategy

The company is strategically focused to lead the petroleum industry using a portfolio which ensures quality net income per barrel, improving returns and operating cash flow growth as the metric.

The strategic objectives of the company are:

- Safety and reliability of operations.
- Marketing fuels and lubricants marketing by investing in higher-returning businesses with higher returns, growth potential and reliable cash flows.
- Efficiency and simplification to maintain and improve competitive advantage.
- Transition to a lower carbon and digitally enabled future over the long term.

A disciplined and well-organised implementation of this strategy will help in the improvement of its performance.

Existing Business Model

A vertically integrated and globally distributed company network with operations in all phases of the oil and gas value chain. Its operations include the exploration and extraction of crude oil and gas, the transportation and trading in oil and gas (in the internal oil and gas market), the manufacturing stage, including refining of fuels, lubricants and petrochemicals, and, ultimately marketing and sales activities which involve selling the refined petrol through numerous service stations globally. The first two stages in the value chain are categorised as "upstream" activities, the last two stages are seen as "downstream" activities, while transportation and trading are known as "midstream" activities.

Discovering Oil and Gas

New discoveries enable the company to renew their portfolio, discover more resources and improve their growth options. The company focuses their exploration activities in competitive the areas, using technology for cost and risk reduction.

Extracting and Producing Oil and Gas

Value is created by improving hydrocarbon resources and turning them into proved reserves if they fit the strategic objectives of the company or selling them if they do not. The resources produced are sold or distributed to their downstream facilities.

Trading and Transporting

The movement of oil and gas is done through pipelines, by trucks, rail and shipment. The company trades many products which include oil, natural gas, liquefied natural gas, power and currencies. Market intelligence is used by the company to analyse global supply and demand for commodities.

Manufacturing and Marketing Fuels and Products

The company produces refined petroleum products at their refineries and supplies distinctive fuel and convenience retail services to consumers through their infrastructure, logistics network and key partnerships.

Generating Renewable Energy

The company operates some biofuel businesses, where low carbon ethanol and low carbon power are produced and also provides renewable power through onshore wind energy and plans to deploy this technology in the wind business in other parts of the worlds to drive efficiency and capacity.

Value Chain Analysis

Employing Michael Porter's model for value chain analysis, the business activities of the oil company can be grouped under two main headings of primary and support activities to identify the activities that the company is best suited to undertake on its own and those it must outsource. Primary activities are those directly linked with the company's creation and delivery of products, while support activities have no direct linkage with production but are responsible for increasing the company's efficiency.

		Inbound Logistics					
Support Activities	Business Infrastructure		Buildings, plants and equipment, IT systems, financial resources				
	Human Resource Management		Involves management of all employees from well to pump				
	Technology Development		Investment in technology throughout the value chain				
	Procurement		Suppliers in high-risk activities are strictly monitored to ensure high safety and quality standards				
Primary Activities	**Extraction**	**Inbound Logistics**	**Operations**	**Outbound Logistics**	**Marketing & Sales**	**Services**	Profit Margin
	Extraction of oil and gas from oil reserves	Includes inventory control, warehousing and materials handling	Activities involved in transforming raw materials into finished products	Storage and distribution of products	Provision of avenues for consumers to purchase products	Value enhancement activities such as repair works	

The value chain reveals the multinational highly heterogeneous network of company with different activities in different stages having different requirements.

Primary Activities

The company's primary activities include research and development into the viability of oil deposits and the extraction of oil and gas, production of fuel and other products, sale and marketing, and services to customers.

Support Activities

The infrastructure to support the primary activities includes buildings, plant and equipment, information technology systems and financial resources. The functions of purchasing inputs are put under the umbrella of procurement. Technology development involves engineering, research and development and process development. Human resource management includes recruitment, training and compensation of all employees.

Value Networks

The value network of the oil company shown below is the intricate web of relationships for the generation of economic value through various complex and dynamic relationships between individuals, groups and companies.

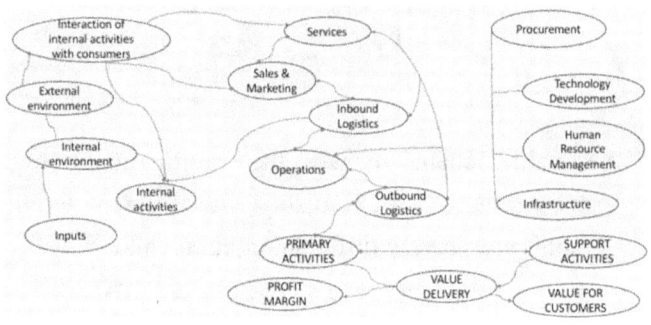

Value-Based Inadequacies Identified and Associated Risks

Inadequacies

The major value-based inadequacy identified in this report was the excessive vertical integration of the petroleum company such that the oil company controls all the stages in its value chain of turning the raw material into finished products and supplying to the customer. Despite the advantages of this strategy such as non-reliance on suppliers, increased economies of scale, better coordination and lower costs of production, its disadvantages far outweigh the benefits. As a forward vertically integrated oil and gas company, value-based inadequacies identified, which must be addressed urgently were:

(i) Huge capital requirements.

(ii) Unbalanced output at the various stages of production or distribution.

(iii) Reduced flexibility in adapting to technological changes and inability to follow consumer trends, and unavailable managerial expertise.

Measures for Value Chain Enhancement

The advanced value chain analysis and the value-based knowledge network identified the following proposed steps as necessary for the enhancement of the company's value chain.

1. There is the need for an IT system aimed at increasing safety in the highly risky petroleum industry. This recovery strategy will boost investor confidence in the company.

2. The company must sell off its downstream operations and concentrate on the upstream as upstream assets attract higher investment rates to revenue generation.

3. The company's market share of can be increased through mergers and acquisitions as oil well continue to dry up globally.

4. The petroleum company must cut costs to increase growth.

5. Transfer resources to alternative energy which has the potential for growth.

Necessary Changes to Existing Business Model to Create Value

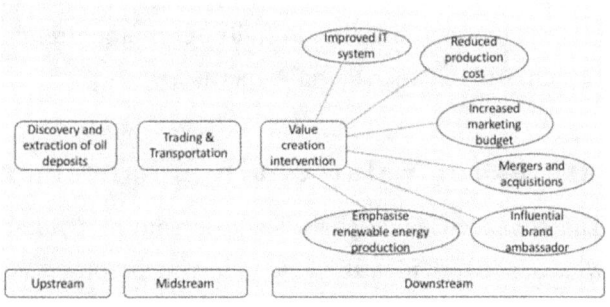

Value Creation Interventions through Stakeholders

The key stakeholders are the suppliers, competitors, customers, shareholders, employees, local communities, academics, media and non-governmental organisations (NGOs). The table below details how each of these key stakeholders can contribute to the value-creation drive of the petroleum company.

Stakeholder	Intervention
Suppliers	Deepen relationship with suppliers to ensure continuous supply of resources.
Competitors	Performance of competitors must serve as a catalyst for better output.
Customers	Customer satisfaction goals can drive value creation.
Shareholders	Shareholders who avoid selling off their investments during challenging times contribute to maintaining the value of the company.
Employees	Employees must appreciate their contribution to the value creation process and work towards it.
Local Communities & NGOs	Social value creation for communities through corporate social responsibility (CSR) interventions in conjunction with NGOs.
Media	Channel rebranding campaign through social and traditional media.

To redeem the lost brand equity and value, the company must employ a strategic marketing plan by taking the following measures:

(i) Appointing an influential brand ambassador.
(ii) Changing the brand positioning of the company to reflect a strong commitment to safety.
(iii) Increasing the marketing budget to accommodate these new measures.

Impact of Proposed Strategic Initiative on the Company's Strategic Positioning

The proposed strategic initiatives will rebrand the company as committed to ensuring safety to regain its lost brand equity and value through the implementation of the new IT system. To mitigate against the risk of drying oil wells due to over usage, a merger with or the acquisition of smaller petroleum companies will ensure the supply of the raw material. Cost cutting measures and the transfer of resources to alternative energy with a high growth projection will increase the income growth of the company, while the sale of the downstream business will concentrate efforts at the upstream where returns are higher. The inclusion of stakeholders in this value creation drive will harness their contributions in diverse forms.

These proposed strategies will create value for business by giving birth to a new company to be known for its commitment to safety, regained brand equity and value.

Chapter Three
Manage the Value Created

*Beware of little expenses; a small leak will sink
a great ship.*
– Warren Buffet

The value created by an organisation or a business must be managed effectively to avoid value erosion.

Value management concerns the improvement of performance analysis with a focus on better housekeeping to improve cash flows as well as the improvement and maintenance of an appropriate balance between the wants and needs of stakeholders and the resources needed to satisfy them. The value judgements of stakeholders vary. Therefore, value management must reconcile opposing priorities to deliver best value for all stakeholders. This is hinged on principles of defining and adding measurable value, focusing on objectives, and concentrating on purpose to enhance innovation. This requires a combination of value focused management style, a positive approach to individual and team motivation, a consciousness of the organisational environment and the effective use of verified approaches and tools.

The value management concept, which was initially introduced into manufacturing for the comparison of different materials to arrive at one which provides the best function at the lowest cost, has gained popularity in other sectors (Shen & Yu, 2012).

Core Concepts and Practices for Value Management

The core concepts and practices for value management include the following:

- Risk management assessment.
- Corporate governance assessment.
- Quantitative analysis.
- Business process improvement.
- Total quality management.

Risk Management Assessment

Institutions are exposed to various types of risk such as credit, market, liquidity, capital, operational, reputational and regulatory risks. In order to avoid loss of income arising from any of the risks faced, a framework must be put in place to manage the risks. Risk management is the identification, assessment and classification of the key risks that a company is exposed to. This helps to provide the best mitigation against the identified risks to avoid losses. The ability of a company to manage its risks must be assessed frequently using competitors and industry standards as benchmarks. Most companies are expected to have a risk management committee who are ultimately responsible for setting the risk appetite of the company.

Enterprise Risk Management (ERM)

Enterprise risk management (ERM) is a continuing process designed to manage all risks within an enterprise and is defined by the Commission of Sponsoring Organisation of the Treadway Commission (COSO) as:

'A process effected by an entity's board of directors, management and other personnel, applied in strategy setting and across the enterprise, designed to identify potential events that may affect the entity, and manage risk to be within its risk appetite, to provide reasonable assurance regarding the achievement of entity objectives'.

It is therefore important to establish an ERM system because it enables a firm to gain a clear interpretation of its total risk level.

Corporate Governance Assessment

Corporate governance is the system by which companies are directed and controlled. Boards of directors are responsible for the governance of their companies. The shareholders' role in governance is to appoint the directors and the auditors and to satisfy themselves that an appropriate governance structure is in place. The responsibilities of the board include setting the company's strategic aims, providing the leadership to put them into effect, supervising the management of the business and reporting to shareholders on their stewardship. Corporate governance is therefore about what the board of a company does and how it sets the values of the company, and it is to be distinguished from the day to day operational management of the company by full-time executives.

In the United Kingdom (UK), the Financial Reporting Council (FRC) is responsible for promoting high quality corporate governance and reporting to foster investment. It does this by bench-marking the operations of the board against set rules known as the corporate governance code which assesses the performance of the board in relation to leadership, effectiveness, accountability, remuneration and relations with shareholders.

Quantitative Analysis

Quantitative analysis of available data helps to obtain comparable and useful results to assess the company against competition and industry. Some useful metrics for quantitative analysis includes Price-Earning (PE) ratio, Return on Capital Employed (ROCE), Return on Equity (ROE), current ratio and gearing ratio.

Price-Earning (PE) Ratio

The PE ratio which is calculated as PE Ratio = Share Price/Earnings per share, is used to measure a company's value by measuring its share price against the earnings per share. If the market considers a company to have good prospects, this usually leads to an increase in the share price (the numerator) which causes the PE ratio to rise.

Return on Capital Employed (ROCE)

The ROCE measures the profitability of a company by measuring the pre-tax profit against the total capital employed (shareholder's funds and borrowings/loans). The higher the ROCE, the more profitable a company.

Return on Equity (ROE)

Return on equity is the ratio of net profit to shareholders' equity (also called book value, net assets or net worth) expressed as a percentage. A measure of how well a company uses shareholders' funds to generate a profit. ROE reveals the profit a company has generated from the funds provided by shareholders. A higher ROE is indicative of a more profitable company.

Calculated as the net income returned as a percentage of the shareholders equity, ROE is also a measure of the profitability of a bank.

Gearing Ratio

The gearing ratio is a financial ratio which compares the shareholder's funds to loans acquired by the company. This is used to measure the ability of a company to survive in an economic decline. This ratio mirrors the amount of shareholder's equity which will be required to pay off all outstanding debts. It will be easier for a company with a lower gearing to pay off debt as compared to companies with gearing ratios of above 50%. High-geared companies represent a greater risk because the slightest incidence of reduced profits could result bankruptcy and loan default.

Improving Business Processes

Business Process Improvement (BPI) is helps companies and enterprises to restructure their existing business operations to achieve significant improvement in products and services. When BPI is effective, it helps to generate reliable results in operational efficiency and focus on customers. The implementation of BPI helps companies to improve the quality of their products or services.

There are many ways of improving a business process, but the key steps involved are:

1. Define process by setting a vision and its strategies.
2. Measure the process by finding the Key Performance Indicators (KPIs).
3. Analyse process by finding the critical success factors.
4. Execute the action plan.

Total Quality Management (TQM)

Ross (1999) defines TQM as 'a cohesive philosophy of management practices which highlights, inter alia, continuous improvement, satisfying customers' needs, reducing repetition, long-term planning, increased teamwork and employee engagement, process design, competitive benchmarking, team-based problem-solving, continuous results monitoring, and supplier relationships'. In other words, it is a management approach to achieving long-term success by focusing on customer satisfaction that is based on the principle that every employee must be committed to maintaining high standards of work in all aspects of a company's operations.

Application

A multinational financial institution with a £700,000 million asset has been in existence for decades. However, its share price has been falling over the last five years prompting stakeholder agitation.

A situational analysis involving 5Cs and CAMELS analysis can be employed to identify the problem areas and make the value of the company. To do this, a situational analysis will be performed using the 5Cs analysis together with a CAMELS analysis to identify the reasons for the erosion of value. This will then lead to appropriate measures to be taken to salvage the value of the financial institution.

5Cs Analysis

This is an all-inclusive analysis of capturing all appropriate information and internal and external factors which affect a company. To analyse the situation of the organisation. Situation analysis is done mostly for strategic decision making because the organisation must first know the current situation so that decisions on the future direction are not only based on impressions and theories which have not been proven. This helps organisations to collect information about their strengths, weaknesses, opportunities and threats. The 5Cs model covers the company, the climate in which it operates, competitors, customers and collaborators of the company.

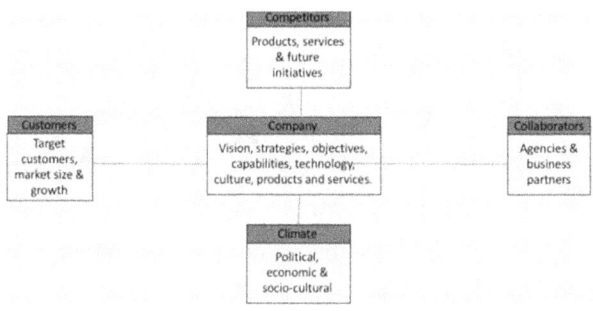

CAMELS Analysis

CAMELS which is an acronym for **c**apital adequacy, **a**sset quality, **m**anagement, earnings, **l**iquidity and sensitivity. It is an internationally recognised rating system for assessing the overall condition of a bank. The scale is from 1 to 5 with 1 being the strongest and 5 the weakest.

Camel Parameter	Ratio
Capital Adequacy	Tier 1 common capital ratio (CET1)
Asset Quality	Asset quality ratio
Management	Profit per employee ratio
Earnings	Growth in net profit
Liquidity	Current ratio
Sensitivity	Net interest margin

Capital Adequacy

This is the minimum statutory reserve banks are expected to keep and gives depositors the confidence that the bank has the ability to meet any additional capital needs. It is measured by many ratios including the Tier 1 common capital ratio, which is a measurement of a bank's core equity capital compared with its total risk-weighted assets that signifies a bank's financial strength.

Asset Quality

Banks are concerned with the quality of the assets on their balance sheets because bad assets such as non-performing loans reduce their income. The asset quality (loan loss) ratio measures the loan impairment for the year as a percentage of loans and advances to customers.

Management

The efficiency of management is also vital. The profit per employee is a good indicator of the management efficiency.

Profit per employee = Profit after tax/No. of employees

Earnings

This determines the profitability of a bank and its future growth in earnings. It was measured with the interest income to total income ratio because interest income is a basic earner.

Liquidity

Liquidity is the extent to a company is able to meet its short-term obligations. The current ratio measures the total current assets against the total current liabilities.

Sensitivity

Sensitivity to market risk refers to the risk that changes in market conditions could negatively affect earnings or capital or both. Since interest rate risk the primary risk faced by most banks, the net interest margin is a good measure.

An example of the CAMELS analysis of the bank under review (Bank 1) with 2 other banks is shown in the table below:

CAPITAL	Capital Adequacy (CET1) (%)	Rank	Average
	Bank 1	2	11.96
	Bank 2	3	10.82
	Bank 3	1	12.50
ASSET	Asset Quality Ratio (%)		
	Bank 1	1	0.39
	Bank 2	3	0.17
	Bank 3	2	0.20
MANAGEMENT	Profit per Employee (£)		

	Bank 1	2	16,673.94
	Bank 2	3	8,924.27
	Bank 3	1	44,453.18
EARNINGS	**Growth in Net Profit (%)**		
	Bank 1	3	62.18
	Bank 2	1	1,272.63
	Bank 3	2	18.07
LIQUIDITY	**Current Ratio**		
	Bank 1	1	2.57
	Bank 2	3	0.89
	Bank 3	2	1.57
SENSITIVITY	**Net Interest Margin(£m)**		
	Bank 1	3	7,932.72
	Bank 2	2	10,026.00
	Bank 3	1	23,476.10

Findings of Situational Analysis

The situational analysis performed using the 5Cs model revealed that although the financial institution had a strong customer base and a large market share, adequate liquidity, and asset quality, the institution required improvement in capital adequacy, management, earnings and sensitivity. The financial analysis of the bank's revealed a decreasing PE ratio, decreasing trend of ROCE, decreasing trend of ROE with records of negative ratios, higher gearing ratio as compared to competition, the need for a more comprehensive risk management strategy, need for improvement in capital, management, earnings and sensitivity.

The value of the financial institution can therefore be managed by:

- Improving operating income by growing revenue, reducing operating cost and rationalising capital expenditure.
- Improving business processes.
- Implementing the Total Quality Management (TQM) and the new strategic management system.
- Adoption of the performance pyramid for the implementation of the new strategic management system.

1. Improving Operating Income

Operating income can be improved by:

(i) Increasing the operating profit.
(ii) Decreasing the weighted average cost of capital.
(iii) Both (i) and (ii)

A strategic financial objective to increase operating income (increasing operating profit and reducing operating cost) the next 3 financial objectives can be achieved as shown in the table below:

i.   Net Revenue Growth.
ii. Operating Cost Reduction.
iii. Capital Expenditure Rationalisation.

Key Value Drivers	Strategic Action Needed	Specification Actions
Net Revenue Growth	Price adjustments	Tariff increment on services
	Re-segmentation of markets	Close loss-making units.
	Sales promotion	Sales promo to increase income from secured lending products (mortgage and auto).
Operating Cost Reduction	Processes efficiency improvements	More efficient loan approval processes to reduce non-performing loans.
	Workforce resource engineering	Centralise processing units in countries with lower staff cost
	Working capital Management	Reduction in employee annual bonuses for 3 years
	Improvements	Reduction in staff cost by outsourcing non-critical services

Capital Expenditure Rationalisation	Review asset acquisition	Lease equipment and official vehicles
		to reduce amortisation costs

2. Improving Business Processes

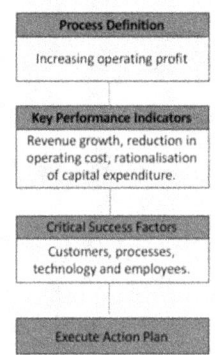

3. Implementation of the Total Quality Management (TQM) System

TQM Strategic Management System

TQM can be applied in this scenario because the financial institution operates in a global market therefore a major distinguishing feature of successful organisations is the quality of leadership, management, employees, work processes, products and services. This requires that products and services must meet customer needs and be provided in unceasingly improving, timely, cost-effective, innovative and productive method. The best system is therefore TQM because it centres on quality and takes a customer-focused approach by involving all employees. This leads to the segregation of roles into value and non-value work and considering non-value work to be less productive.

Vision, mission and values	Employees must appreciate how their roles contribute to the organisational strategy and objectives
Critical Success Factors (CSFs)	Customers, processes, technology and employees
KPI Monitoring	Data collection and analysis
Reward systems	Introduction of employee reward systems
Feedback	Customer surveys
Remedial Actions	Address any negative feedback

The TQM system focuses on:

- Continuously making the reason for quality improvement known to employees.
- Removing unnecessary hierarchies within the company by getting every employee to be committed (total employee involvement).
- Ensuring employees are trained for quality improvement.
- Increasing customer satisfaction and loyalty by improving performance.
- Fact-based decision making.
- Strategic and systematic approach.
- An integrated system.

Though TQM has been criticised for demanding a lot of resources and not producing tangible improvements, the proposed system for the financial institution will be monitored with analytical and statistical tools to measure tangible improvements in the performance of the company. The profitability over time will make all the resources allocated to the implementation of this system worthwhile.

Chapter Four
Transform the Organisation

Transformation isn't a future event. It's a present-day activity.
— Jillian Michaels

Organisational transformation takes the form of a restructuring or re-engineering of business activities after the gap has been identified. To be successful, these operational changes must be accompanied with changes in employee attitude and the organisational culture.

Causes of underachievement in organisations include inadequate leadership, service delivery, organisational cohesion, strategy execution, poor implementation planning, non-compliant culture and employee disengagement. Corrective measures can be achieved through efficient leadership, risk assessment, value creation efforts demand for accountability from employees.

Identification of the gap requires a critical situational analysis with business models such as the business model canvas and VRIO analysis.

Business Model Canvas

The business model canvas, which was first proposed in 2008 by Alexander Osterwalder, is a structured template tool for business planning. It can be employed for the creation of new business models and the development of existing business models by offering a visual chart which covers the key elements for planning business models. The business model canvas has nine elements, which are listed in the order in which they must be addressed: value proposition, customer segments, channels, customer relationships, revenue streams, key resources, key partners, key activities and cost structure.

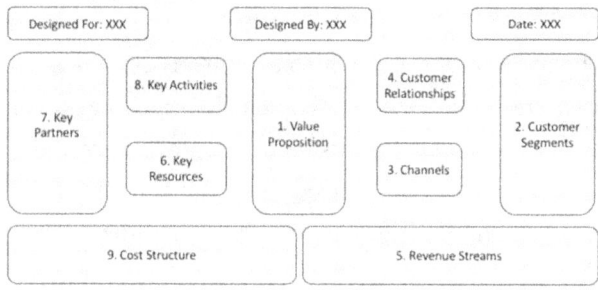

1. Value Proposition

Value proposition refers to the products and/or services that a business offers to satisfy the needs of customers. This concerns the ability of the business to present unique solutions different from other competitors. Value is primarily about problem solving and can be proposed through design, performance, customisation, price, accessibility or technology.

2. Customer Segments

Businesses exist because of customers and must therefore understand their customers' needs for the maximisation of the potential for income generation. This process ensures that the right people are targeted with marketing and communication strategies and customers segmented based on their differing needs, attributes and interests. A business may have one or multiple customer segments depending on the nature of their work. To carry out an effective customer segmentation, a company must first know its customers' needs and list these needs terms of priority.

3. Channels

The medium through which a company provides its value proposition to its customer segments is known as a channel. Once a business develops its value proposition and identifies its customers, there is the need to establish the best channels for the distribution of products and services the fastest, most efficient and most cost-effective way. These may include virtual channels such as websites and physical channels such as a distributor.

4. Customer Relationships

Finding, keeping and growing a customer base must be a key to every business, since customers ensure the survival of every business. Strategies must therefore be identified by businesses to maintain a positive, long-term relationship with customers.

5. Revenue Streams

Businesses need to identify how to make money from each customer segment and understand the profitability of each segment in order commit the appropriate resources to each segment.

6. Key Resources

The resources needed to make the business model work must be identified. These resources may include human, financial, equipment and infrastructure, and time.

7. Key Partners

This refers to external organisations the business intends to partner to deliver its value proposition and make the model work. These partners may include suppliers, buyers, subsidiaries, joint ventures, and alliances with other businesses.

8. Key Activities

At this stage, the key activities needed to take place for the business plan progress must be identified. That is, the activities and tasks needed to be performed to implement the value proposition and reach the identified customers.

9. Cost Structure

The concluding section of the business model canvas is associated with the financial aspect of the business. Exploring the cost structure ensures that the business understands what costs and expenditure will need to be covered. These may include fixed and variable costs and expenditure.

Benefits of the Business Model Canvas

The use of the business model canvas in planning business activities has numerous benefits including:

(i) Provision of a comprehensive overview of the key topics to ensure that no fundamental elements are omitted from the plan.

(ii) It can be used for all businesses including big, small, new or established ones.

(iii) Provision of clear guidance and direction for beginners in business planning.

(iv) Aids visual thinking by providing a neat breakdown of the major considerations impacting the business.

Limitations of the Business Model Canvas

The major limitations of the business model canvas are as follows:

1. It excludes the organisation's mission, vision and strategic objectives.

2. It does not take into account the notion of competition.

3. Key Performance Indicators (KPIs) and performance measurement are omitted from the model.

4. The Canvas somehow suggests that only financial success can drive business. This cannot be true for social enterprises and non-governmental

organisations (European Centre for Research Training and Development UK, 2013).

Once the areas of underachievement have been identified with the Business Model Canvas, the VRIO framework can then be applied to identify and strengthen sources of competitive advantage for the company.

VRIO FRAMEWORK

VRIO is an acronym for valuable, rare, costly to imitate, organised to capture value of resources. The framework is a tool for analysing the internal resources and competences of a company to ascertain if they can be a source of sustained competitive advantage. The tool was originally developed by J.B. Barney, in 1991 and was called VRIN. He identified four features that the resources of a company must possess in order to be a basis of sustained competitive advantage (that is being valuable, rare, imperfectly imitable and non-substitutable). In his later work in 1995, Barney introduced an improvement of the VRIN model known and the VRIN framework. In VRIO analysis four questions are asked to ascertain if a resource is (i) valuable (ii) rare (iii) costly to imitate and (iv) if a firm is organised to seize the opportunity the value of the resources presents. A resource or competence that meets all these four requirements can bring sustained competitive advantage to the company.

The VRIO Framework

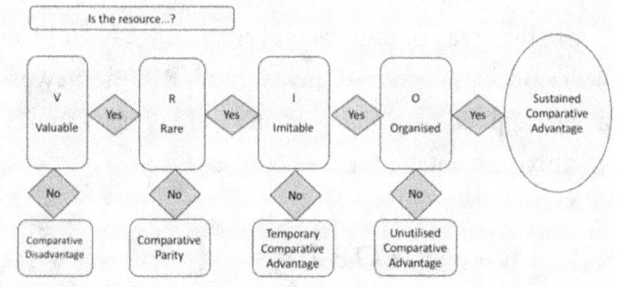

Valuable

If a resource enhances value by enabling a firm to exploit opportunities or defend against threats, then it is valuable. Resources can also be valuable if they help the company to increase customer value. A resource which is not valuable leads to competitive disadvantage.

Rare

Resources and capabilities which can be obtained by only one or a few organisations are considered rare. Rare and valuable resources provide temporary competitive advantage. Competitive parity arises when many organisations possess the same resource or capability due to the fact that firms can utilise similar resources to implement the same strategies with no particular company achieving a higher performance. Even though competitive parity is not the desired position, it is not advisable for firms to neglect the resources that are valuable but common because losing valuable resources and capabilities may adversely affect the organisation because they are vital for staying in the business environment.

Costly to Imitate

A resource is costly to imitate if other organisations do not have it or cannot imitate it, buy or substitute it at a reasonable price. Imitation can occur by directly imitating (duplicating) the resource or providing a comparable product or service (substituting). A firm that has valuable, rare and costly to imitate resources can achieve sustained competitive advantage. Any of the following resources can be difficult to imitate.

- Resources which were developed due to historical events are usually costly to imitate.
- The resources and capabilities that are built on the organisation's culture or interpersonal relationships.

Organised to Capture Value

Resources and capabilities do not provide any benefit for a company unless they are organised to capture the value from them. A company must therefore organise its culture, organisational structure, processes, management systems, and policies to fully attain the full potential of its valuable, rare and costly to imitate resources and capabilities. It is only then that sustained competitive advantage can be achieved.

Using the VRIO Framework

1. Identifying valuable, rare and costly to imitate resources

Resources can be classified as being tangible or intangible. Tangible resources are physical such as landed property and equipment and can easily be purchased in the market. Therefore, tangible resources are seldom a source of competitive advantage. Intangible assets, in contrast, such as brand reputation, intellectual property, trademarks, unique training system or unique way of performing tasks, cannot easily be acquired and provide the benefits of sustained competitive advantage. Companies must therefore protect their intangible assets since they are usually the valuable, rare and costly to imitate resources. The questions listed below can be helpful in the identification of valuable resources.

Identifying Valuable Resources

i. Which activities increase product or service differentiation and perceived customer value?
ii. Which activities reduce the cost of production without diminishing perceived customer value?
iii. Does the business have access to any scarce raw materials?
iv. Do your employees have unique skills and capabilities?
v. Does the company have brand reputation for quality, innovation or customer service?
vi. Does the company have any other strength compared to the competition?

Identifying Rare Resources

i.   Can the resource be easily acquired in the market by competitors now or on future?

ii. How many other companies own the same resource the industry?

Identifying Costly to Imitate Resources

i.   Can other companies easily duplicate the resource or its substitute?

ii. Is the resource protected by a patent?

iii. Is a resource or capability socially complex?

2. Is the company is organised to exploit these resources identified

The following questions can be helpful in this process.

1. Does the company have an effective strategic management process?

2. Is there an effective motivation and reward system in place?

3. Does the company encourage innovative ideas from employees?

4. Are there efficient control systems?

3. Protect the resources identified

The next stage after the identification of resources or capabilities that possess all the four VRIO attributes is to ensure that they are protected because they form the basis of the sustained competitive advantage of the organisation. These resources can be protected legally through trademarks, patents, and copyrights.

4. Constantly review VRIO resources and capabilities

Resources must be review constantly to ascertain if they are still valuable since value of resources changes over time. If competitors are able to achieve the same competitive advantages by replicating a company's resources, the rarity of the resource will be eroded.

Application

The airline is one of the main airlines in the United Kingdom with a large aircraft fleet and a large customer base. However, the airline has experienced some industrial actions from disgruntled employees over remuneration.

A situational analysis revealed the following:

1. A quantitative analysis revealed that an increase in the head count of the airline company was not accompanied with a corresponding increase in the total employee cost.

2. The business model canvas revealed unreasonable cost cutting measures and poor employee management.
3. VRIO analysis

	Valuable?	Rare?	Costly to imitate?	Exploited by the organisation?	Competitive implication?	Economic implication?
of planes	Yes	Yes	Yes	Yes	SCA	AN
	Yes	Yes	Yes	Yes	SCA	AN
	Yes	Yes	Yes	Yes	SCA	AN
ess Channels	Yes	Yes	Yes	Yes	SCA	AN
isational Culture	Yes	Yes	Yes	Yes	SCA	AN
gic Partners	Yes	Yes	Yes	Yes	SCA	AN
ctual Property	Yes	Yes	Yes	Yes	SCA	AN
mer Service Quality	Yes	Yes			UCA	UIC
mer Relationships	Yes	Yes			UCA	UIC
nation Systems	Yes	Yes			TCA	TAN
gy	Yes	Yes			TCA	TAN
ue Streams	Yes				CP	N
ess Environment	Yes				CP	N
d & Experienced Staff	Yes				CD	
lyee Relationships	Yes				CD	

Legend for VRIO Analysis Table

1. Sustained Competitive Advantage = SCA
2. Unexploited Competitive Advantage = UCA
3. Temporary Competitive Advantage = TCA
4. Competitive Parity = CP
5. Competitive Disadvantage = CD
6. Above Normal = AN
7. Unused Incurred cost = UIC
8. Temporarily Above Normal = TAN
9. Normal = N

Summary of VRIO Analysis

(i)   The airline's fleet of planes, slots, brand, business channels, organisational culture, strategic partners and intellectual property were a source of sustained competitive advantage, implying an "above normal" economic implication.

(ii) Customer service quality and customer relationships and information technology systems immerged as temporary competitive advantage.

(iii) The revenue streams of the airline and its business environment made it at par with its competitors.

(iv) Relationships with trained and experienced staff were a source of competitive disadvantage to the aviation company.

Proposed Strategic Actions for Organisational Transformation

i.   Improve management/employee relations

The unrest between management and the staff over remuneration can be improved by benchmarking their conditions of service against the industry average and airlines in the same category. The company must ensure that staff is at par with their contemporaries in other airline companies. The company can also consider outsourcing the recruitment and human resource management in order to concentrate on other areas.

ii.   Efficient cost cutting

The airline can cut cost to increase profitability by outsourcing non-critical areas. However, critical areas such as the information technology systems, on which many other operations are hinged, should be under the direct control and management of the airline irrespective of the cost involved.

Chapter Five
Embrace Innovation and Change

Changes call for innovation, and innovation leads to progress.
– Li Keqiang

The pace at which technology is advancing requires businesses to constantly transition to new and better processes or risk being left behind by the competitive environment. Organisations need constant innovation to succeed in staying ahead of competition with better business strategies and processes. This requires policies to be implemented to put innovation at the forefront of business innovation.

Depending on the problems identified, innovation and change can be achieved with the implementation of Lewin's Change Model, Kotter's 8 stages of change, the Genome and the Pentathlon Models.

To be successful at innovation, businesses must be able to manage change and sustain competitive advantage.

Lewin's Change Model

Kurt Lewin is the originator of the 3-step change model (Cummings & Huse, 1989). Lewin (1947) reasoned that a real change project was made up of three stages which are unfreezing, moving or changing and refreezing and suggested that human behavioural stability depended on a semi-static balance supported by an intricate field of powerful and limiting forces. He therefore argued that the balance needs to be subverted (unfrozen) before old conduct can be cast-off (unlearnt) and a new one adopted successfully. Schein (1996) asserts that unfreezing is not the culmination but rather generates the enthusiasm to learn without controlling or predicting the direction, which resonates Lewin's view. The last stage of the 3-step model is "refreezing" where the organisation is re-stabilised at a new semi-stationary state to ensure the new behaviours are free from retrogression.

Lewin's change model is very rational and goal oriented.

It is also simple to use as it involves three steps which can easily be followed through, thereby making planning for change easier and addresses any potential opposition by addressing such difficulties head on.

Though the Lewin's change model appears rational, the lack of consideration of human feelings and experiences during implementation has the potential of resulting in negative consequences, Kristonis (2004–2005). According to Hoogendoorn (2013), problems may arise during the refreezing stage where employees may have concerns about the impending change and may therefore not be as productive as expected.

Kotter's 8 Stages of Change

John Kotter (1996) of Harvard University advanced a more comprehensive approach for change management by building on the foundation laid by Kurt Lewin (Lunenburg, 2010). To begin, Kotter listed common mistakes leaders make in an attempt to bring about change. These errors included giving room for too much complacency, failure to create a strong coalition for change management, lack of vision for change, ineffective communication of the vision for change, obstacles that block the vision, failure to create short-term successes, premature declaration of victory, failure to imbibe changes into organisational culture (Kotter 1996). With these errors in mind, Kotter (2012) then proposed an eight-step method for the management of change as follows:

i. Establish a sense of urgency.
ii. Create the guiding coalition.
iii. Develop a vision and strategy.
iv. Communicate the change vision.
v. Empower employees for broad-based action.
vi. Generate short-term wins.
vii. Consolidate gains and produce more change.
viii. Anchor new approaches in the culture.

Though Kotter's 8-step model lacks rigorous rudiments, it has been well accepted and has remained a pivotal mark in the literature on change management (Appelbaum, et al., 2012). The model, which was not intended for all types of change, works well on essential changes in the way that businesses must be run to handle a new and more demanding situation (Kotter 1995).

Kotter's model of change management does not have rigorous fundamentals (Appelbaum, 2012) and might not be applicable to all types of change scenarios. Kotter encourages the 8 steps to be followed sequentially since overlapping or omitting steps may compromise the success. However, Burnes (1996) contends that this kind of a rigid style does not help many organisations and many studies have suggested that organisations prefer approaches to change which are based on their own organisational culture. Sidorko (2008); Penrod and Harbor (1998) also point out that the implementation and evaluation of all the eight steps is a difficult process.

The Innovation Genome

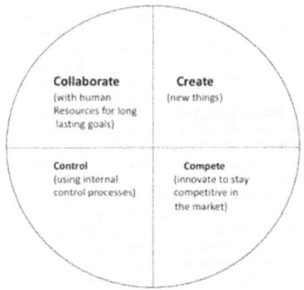

Jeff Degraff describes the Innovation Genome as a map or meta-model for the comparison and evaluation of innovation approaches. He further explained it as a tool for the synchronisation of the immense horizontal functions of complex organisations as innovation is basically a horizontal value proposition. The three levels of innovation and the four fundamental creative forces are the two basic operational mechanisms of the innovation genome.

The three levels of innovation which are the "purpose", "practices" and "personal" are interrelated like Russian nesting dolls where each level is incorporated into the other and no level can create value on its own.

The four fundamental forces which are "collaborate", "create", "compete", and "control" drive innovation in dyadic oppositions with "collaborate" against "compete" and "create" against "control". It can be used in many areas in an organisation including changing organisational culture; improvement in performance management processes and the creation of shared visions and values. Due to the interconnectivity of the three levels, each level can draw on the strengths of the others to make up for its weaknesses.

However, according to critics, since the innovation is fairly new, it will have to undergo more trials to identify its flaws however it has been identified the it is cumbersome to use and requires a lot of practice from users for perfection to be achieved.

The Pentathlon Model

Goffin and Pfeiffer (1999) and Oke and Goffin (2001) define the Pentathlon model as 'a general framework for the management of innovation which addresses many soft organisational issues'. According to Goffin and Pfeiffer (1999), to realise effective innovation management, organisations must perform well in five areas integrated areas as shown in the diagram below.

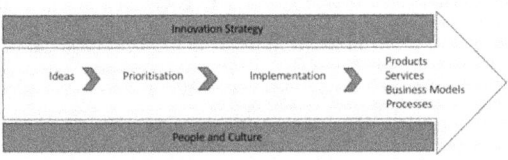

The pentathlon framework offers a structure for the management of innovation within an organisation by creating the opportunity for the recognition of the strengths and weaknesses, which when correctly applied helps with innovation for solutions. The pentathlon model also helps with the structuring of an organisation's innovation processes on five linked areas, none of which can be neglected (Mitchell, 2011).

One major flaw identified by critics is the lack of linkage between the model and the organisation's strategic objectives (Goffin Keith & Mitchell Rick, 2005).

Application

An airline company is noted for its relatively inexpensive airfare and rapid expansion due its cheaper air travel business model. With a large fleet of aircrafts, the airline operates thousands of flights daily from various airport bases and connects many destinations in different countries. A large crew of expert aviation specialists enable the airline to deliver its splendid performance. However, a recent mismanagement of the airline's employee leave system resulted in a cancelation of numerous flights and subsequent huge losses to the company.

A situational analysis with SWOT, McKinsey's 7s Analysis and the Business Model Canvas revealed the following:

Business Model Canvas

The business model canvas analysis revealed a tight business model where the airline aims to deliver low-cost airline services whiles paying charges and fees to airport companies and receiving subsidies and support from the airports. The main value proposition of the airline was low-cost fares by offering prices about 20% lower than competitors.

Summary of SWOT Analysis

From the SWOT analysis, the airline has a strong brand name, an established market share, a strong balance sheet and low distribution cost. The main weakness identified was weak employee relations which led to the mismanagement of the leave system. The threat to the company is increasing airport charges and fuel price volatility. Market growth in the aviation industry proves to be a good opportunity for the airline which must therefore take advantage of its strengths, change its weaknesses, manage its threats and leverage on its opportunities.

Summary of McKinsey's 7s Analysis

It was identified that apart from systems and style, no other components required any changes apart from the need to implement a new HR system to monitor staff leave periods and holidays.

Proposed Strategic Actions for Innovation and Change

Lewin's Change Model

Based on the results of the situational analysis the need for efforts aimed at overcoming any resistance to change, development of new attitudes and behaviours, change implementation and the consolidation of the change was realised. The Kurt Lewin's Change Model to unfreeze, change and refreeze the system of the airline (Robbins, 2003).

Stage	Characteristics	Organisational Impact
Unfreeze	Build confidence in staff and appreciation for the need for change (Kritsonis, 2004) by organising staff to explain the need for a change in the leave management system by highlighting the setbacks of the current system and the advantages of the proposed system.	This will reduce or eliminate any antagonism once staff appreciates the benefits of the consultant's work.

Change	Introduce change to employees through training programmes to convince them that the current situation is not beneficial to them (Kritsonis, 2004) because the huge financial losses during the peak of the crises could have been channelled into staff welfare.	This will resolve any reservations employees have about the change.
Refreeze	Create an acceptance for change by incorporating change into the daily routines of staff. Staff who makes quick progress must be rewarded.	This step must be taken to prevent employees from reverting to the old system (Goode, 2008).

Change and Innovation

Innovation must play a critical role if any proposed change can be successfully implemented. The innovation genome and the pentathlon model of innovation can be employed for this purpose.

Kotter's 8 Stages of Change

Kotter's 8 stages can be applied to the airline situation as follows:

i.   Establish the importance of a properly managed leave system.

ii.   Create a coalition of change and innovation ambassadors to champion the process.

iii. Develop a vision and strategy for change and innovation.

iv.   Communicate the vision and strategy.

v.   Empower employees through training and removal of barriers.

vi.   Split change process into measurable stages for assessment and celebration of short-term wins.

vii. Consolidate gains and produce more changes.

viii. Anchor new approaches in the organisational culture and encourage staff to embrace the change process as a daily routine.

Genome Model

The innovation genome has two structural components, can be used to coordinate the vast horizontal functions of the airline across regional and functional boundaries. These components are:

i.   The three level of innovation.

ii.   The four fundamental creative forces.
      (Degraff & Quinn, 2006)

The 3 Levels of Innovation

The three levels of the innovation genome comprise the purposes, practices and personal are inter-related like Russian nesting dolls where each level is subsumed by the greater level. The airline purposes to create a seamless leave management system for employees while maintaining its cost-cutting practice. This will require leaders with personal ambitions of the willingness to support the innovation process.

The Four Fundamental Creative Forces

The four fundamental forces of collaboration, creation, control, and competition can help the airline to invest in Information technology for the creation of innovative ways of employee management through collaboration with staff while the leverage of low-cost airfares continues.

Pentathlon Model

In order not to be limited to one aspect of innovation management, a broader view can be taken by considering a wider range of issues which were the generation of ideas for innovation; selection, prioritisation and implementation of the ideas generated; innovation and strategy; and the business culture of the Airline (Goffin & Mitchell, 2016)

McKinsey's 7s Framework

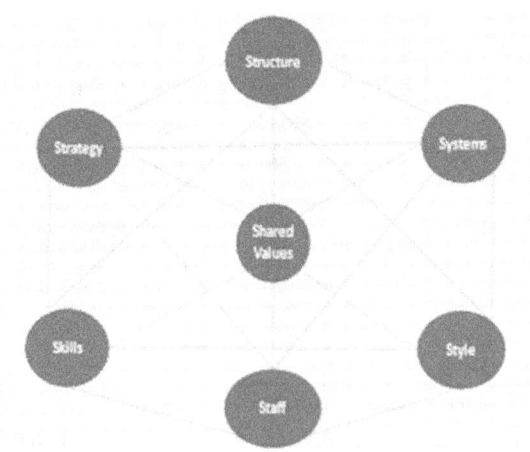

The framework helps organisations to know how well they are positioned for the achievement of their goals. It is useful for examining how the different parts of the organisation work together.

The seven elements are categorised as hard or soft with the hard elements being strategy, structure and systems; and the soft elements being shared values, skills, style and staff.

The hard elements can be easily identified and can be directly influenced by management. On the other hand, the soft elements are more difficult to describe and are more influenced by the culture of the organisation.

Usually, the framework is used when the effectiveness and the design of the organisation are in question.

The components of the McKinsey's 7s framework are listed in the table below:

Strategy	Plan developed by the organisation to sustain competitive advantage.
Structure	The way units are organised with the institution, indicating the reporting lines. This is also known as organisational structure.
Systems	The daily activities, processes and procedures within the company.
Skills	Abilities of the employees of the firm.
Staff	Type and number of employees in a company.
Style	Management style of the leaders of the company.
Shared Values	This is at the core of the model and represents the standards that guide the behaviour of employees.

To use this model, the following steps must be followed:

1. Identification of areas that are not effectively aligned to each other.
2. Determination of the best organisational design.
3. Decide areas needing change.
4. Make the changes.
5. Continuous review of the 7s.

Proposed Solution

With the tight business model, the best solution to the absence management problem will be the implementation of a good internet-based absence management system which will allow the human resource management team of to document and track everything through the online system. Additionally, it will be prudent for the management of the airline company to employ the services of a leadership consultant to work with the chief executive officer on his leadership style.

Holidays of staff of the airline can be booked a simple and user-friendly interface and approved within seconds on the new system and the holiday calendar will allow management to see who is off at what time.

Management of Sick Leave

Records of short-term and long-term illnesses will be kept by the system and the Bradford Factor (formula used in human resource management for measuring employee absenteeism) scores of employees for the identification of trends and issues.

The system will produce reports for various forms of absenteeism; generate alerts for pending requests for approval and when staff returns to work.

The system can be accessed from anywhere once there is internet connectivity.

Benefits of Implementing Proposed Solution

i.   Efficient use of the system will have huge financial benefits by reducing unplanned absenteeism.
ii. It will avoid leave clashes and staff shortages during peak periods.
iii. The use of one system will create consistency and synchronisation in the management of absenteeism.

iv. Employees will be empowered to log in their absences due to the accessibility of the system.

Chapter Six
Effective Leadership

A leader is one who sees more than others see, who sees farther than others see, and who sees before others see.
— **Leroy Eimes**

Leadership Defined

There are many definitions of leadership however, Peter G. Northouse (*Leadership, Theory and Practice, 7th Edition*) defines leadership as 'a process where an individual influences a group of people to achieve a common goal'. Peter goes on to explain that instead of being seen as a trait or characteristic residing in an individual, leadership is rather a transactional event between the leader and his followers. He also described leadership as a process since the leader affects and is also affected by his followers.

The above definition of leadership ensures that it is available to all and not restricted to certain individuals with certain character traits or one formally assigned with the responsibility of leading a group.

Other definitions of leadership are:

Leadership is the ability of an individual to influence, motivate and enable others to contribute towards the effectiveness and success of the organisations of which they are members (House, et al., 2004).

Leadership is an influence relationship among leaders and followers who intend real changes that reflect their shared purposes (Rost, 1993).

Excellent organisations have leaders who shape the future and make it happen, acting as role models for its values and ethics and inspiring trust at all times. They are flexible, enabling the organisation to anticipate and react in a timely manner to ensure the on-going success of the organisation (EQFM, 2013).

All the definitions of leadership above stress the theme of interpersonal leadership which is centred around people, goal, change, process and time orientation.

Leadership Styles

A leadership style is the way a leader implements plans, provides direction and motivates people. Different authors have identified many different leadership styles, such as are portrayed by political, corporate and business leaders. There are different types of leadership styles such autocratic, bureaucratic, democratic, charismatic, laissez-faire, people-oriented, task-oriented, servant, transactional and transformational; each leadership styles having its unique traits.

Assessment of Leadership Performance

Leadership performance of the management of the organisation can be assesses based on the idea proposed by the European Foundation for Quality Management (EQFM) Excellence Model that leadership is one of the five enablers that result in people, society, customer and business results. The other four enablers are strategy, people, processes, products and services, and partnerships and resources.

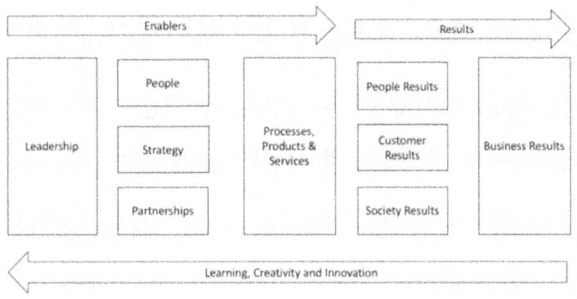

Some people believe that leadership has a visible effect on a team or an organisation. However, this view about the impact of leadership is not shared by all. Alternative views portrayed by the Ritual Scapegoating Theory (RST), the Common-Sense Theory (CST) and the Vicious Cycle Theory (VCT).

❖ According to the ritual scapegoating theory, leadership has no effect on the outcome of an organisation but the replacement of a leader after a series of bad performances pacifies the public who falsely believe in the impact of the leader.

- ❖ The common-sense theory suggests that the replacement of a leader after a bad performance indicates a positive shift in the organisation.
- ❖ The vicious cycle theory proposes that succession is disruptive and bad performance is caused by insufficient organisational efficiency (Rowe & Gorman, 2005).

Balanced Scorecard

The balanced scorecard (BSC) is a strategy performance management tool, which can be used by supervisors for monitoring the performance of their subordinates. The critical characteristics that define a balanced scorecard are:

- Its emphasis on the strategic agenda of the concerned organisation.
- The range of a small number of data items for monitoring.
- A mixture of financial and non-financial data items.

The balanced scorecard was originally intended and used for the measurement of performance in organisations (Kaplan and Norton, 1992). According to Kaplan and Norton (2002), to measure performance in an organisation, the focus must be on the financial, customer, internal process and learning and growth. The measurement of these four metrics helps firms to track all the vital aspects of the strategy of an organisation. However, according to Madsen and Stenheim (2014), for private revenue-generating organisations, financial metrics emphasis on revenue and business growth (market share) whereas for governmental and non-governmental organisations, financial metrics focus on some anticipated result-oriented procedures. The balanced scorecard also measures the perception of customer about the organisation. This perception is important to sustain and increase sales because businesses generate revenue through sales to customers (Casey and Peck, 2004). Kaplan and Norton in 1992 indicated that the customer perspective of the balanced scorecard measures performance, time, cost and quality. Bose and Thomas added to this in 2007 when they stated that the balanced scorecard also measures internal processes by focusing on the actions which boost client satisfaction; innovation and learning for the improvement of employee skills and achievement of better internal business procedure.

Benefits and Limitations of Balanced Scorecard

Kaplan and Norton who are the key proponents of the balanced scorecard asserted in 1992 and 2002 that the strategy tool was beneficial to the implementation of organisations. However, at the inception of the balanced scorecard, Kaplan and Norton indicated that the key benefits were to support organisations for the development and implementation of effective business policies (Kaplan and Norton, 1992). In 2014, Madsen and Stenheim added that, in spite of the numerous academic critiques of the balanced scorecard concerning the connection between the balanced scorecard and performance, its extensive usage suggests that it has some benefits. Additionally, Rigby and Bilodeau (2013) argued that the successful spread of the balanced scorecard amongst numerous organisations nearly two decades after its commencement is sufficient proof that organisations that have implemented it are either satisfied with the tool or find certain aspects of it useful.

Pessanha and Prochnik (2006) stated that the difficulties encountered during execution, high rates of application let-downs and the significant differences in both understanding and practice of the balanced scorecard proves grave limits in both concept and in application. It would be expected that many decades after its inception, the balanced scorecard would have matured and all its teething problems dealt with but this has not been the case as observed by Parmenter (2012). Additionally, in spite of three theoretical revisions and three generations, the concept of the balanced scorecard still faces a considerable amount of critiques (Awadallah & Allam, 2015).

Core Leadership Responsibilities and Functions

John Adair, in his action-centred leadership model (1988), stated that leaders have three main responsibilities and must perform six functions. The responsibilities of leaders as illustrated in the three circles diagram are:

- Achievement of the task.
- Management of a team or group.
- Management of individuals.

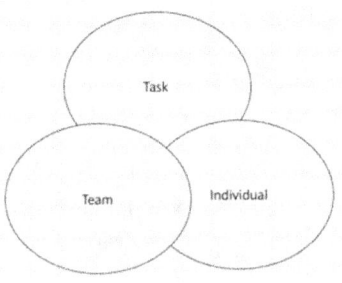

To qualify as good and effective leaders, they must be able to handle all the leadership responsibilities. Many armed forces echo that a leader's main responsibility is task-oriented. However, a task-oriented focus of leadership will alienate followers. Also, leaders who engage in what Blake and Mouton (1964) refer to as "country club" management by focusing on the welfare and psychological issues while neglecting performance will have difficulty meeting set targets. Adair also stated that the main functions of leadership are initiating, planning, informing, controlling, supporting and evaluating.

Prof. Thomas Sergiovanni (1984) also stated that the responsibility of leaders is to be concerned with what is good as well as effective. Good leadership is characterised by exercising charisma and influence over other people for the achievement of a specific goal. The provision of good leadership requires the capability of either performing the assigned tasks or the ability to delegate to other competent people. With a focus on the goal, a good leader must inspire the followers and lead by example. Some essential skills required for good leadership include enthusiasm, integrity, good communication skills, loyalty, mentoring, charisma, competence, decisiveness.

Application

A leading retailer of sports, fashion and fitness products has gone through a quick expansion. This expansion has however been bedevilled with problems as employees have felt the brunt of this expansion drive. The company has been accused of using brutal and autocratic leadership to drive its expansion projects.

A critical analysis of the company identified fear culture, unfavourable wages and salaries and unfair contracts and a gap in the knowledge of core leadership responsibilities and functions.

Improvement Potential and Required Changes

To correct the current state of leadership, there will be the need for the introduction of a balanced scorecard approach to performance management.

The balanced scorecard developed by Kaplan and Norton had four perspectives namely; financial, customer, internal business processes and learning and growth. However, to meet the peculiar need of the company in question, the consultant developed a human resource management scorecard to address the leadership issues confronting the company.

Customising Kaplan and Norton's balanced scorecard to meet the needs of the company. and translate the organisation's vision and mission into operational actions. It can be employed in this case to detect and improve several of its internal functions, specifically the Human Resource (HR) management and provide feedback to the management because it is a good metric for the assessment of the performance in organisations. Adoption of a modern human resource policy. Specification of roles and responsibilities of all employees; Development of a positive organisational culture; and the realignment of organisational strategy will be achieved.

Role	Objective(s)	Metric	Business Value
Modern Human Resource Policy	To eliminate the outmoded policies.	The number of employees who are able to manage their own roles.	Employees become more assertive and better able to manage their own affairs freeing management to take strategic decision.
	Introduce a more balanced approach.		
	Specification of roles and responsibilities.		
Values and Ethics	Employees understand and apply corporate values.	Examination of depth of knowledge of corporate values through surveys and assessments	Development of a positive organisational culture.

Compensation	Compensation must be linked to performance. Fair compensation must be paid to both permanent and outsourced staff.	Salaries of outsourced staff must be commensurate with their work.	Fewer staff agitations and lower staff turn-over rate.
Well-Being	Employees must be fit to perform their roles.	Improvement in the holistic wellbeing of employees.	A happier and content workforce.
Organisational Strategy	The strategy of the organisation must be realigned to adopt a more comprehensive and humanitarian approach.	Targets set for leaders must not only be financial but also include internal processes, learning and growth.	An

i. Adoption of a modern Human Resource (HR) policy

A modern human resource policy will do away with "Victorian" way of managing staff and focus on the improvement of the processes within the company. These modern practices will introduce a more balanced approach which will require the employees to own and manage their roles. The modern HR policy must clearly articulate the vision, mission and values of the organisation, provide effective communication channels and offer training to develop the skills and behaviour of staff in alignment with the vision, mission and values.

ii. Specification of roles and responsibilities of all employees

The specification of roles and responsibilities will eliminate or reduce situations where management fails to accept responsibility for wrong doings in the company. Employees, being aware of reward systems for punctuality and for meeting individual targets, will hopefully perform above expectation. Key Performance Indicators (KPIs) must also be given to each staff for routine assessment of performance and set targets.

iii. Development of a positive organisational culture

Driving efforts into the development of a positive culture in the organisation will eliminate the existing fear culture, increase employee engagement and reduce staff attrition rate.

iv. Realignment of organisational strategy

A realignment of the strategy of the company which has hitherto been skewed towards monetary rewards and contentious methods of business growth. With a balanced scorecard approach, the same results can be achieved through a persuasive, comprehensive and development approach though it may require a little more time.

v. Adoption of a better leadership style

To change the current autocratic leadership style to a more participatory and transformational leadership style, all staff in leadership roles will be required to take self-assessment tests such as the Johari Window self-assessment test and based on the result, undergo the right training for transformation.

The leaders will then be trained to know their core responsibilities of completing their tasks, leading and managing teams and leading and managing individuals.

Their main functions of initiating, planning, controlling, supporting, informing and evaluating their subordinates will also be handled during their training sessions with the consultant.

Finally, the leaders will be taught how to lead and manage themselves to have exemplary characters, be enthusiastic about their work, be confident, stay calm under stress, tolerate divergent views, focus on goals, think analytically and be committed to excellence.

Benefits of the Leadership Development Programme

The model of excellence of the European Foundation for Quality Management (EFQM) states that leadership is one of the five enablers which together with strategy, people, resources and partnerships, products, processes and services lead to results in people, society, customers and businesses (EQFM, 1988). Therefore, the company will have a happier and more productive workforce if the leadership development programme proposed above is implemented. This will gradually change the negative image that the company has for the management of employee related issues. Additionally, the loss of skilled labour to competitors will be minimised if not completely stopped.

Chapter Seven
Strategy

Strategy is about setting yourself apart from the competition. It's not a matter of being better at what you do—it's a matter of being different at what you do.
– Michael Porter

The consequences of managing a business without a comprehensive strategy can be dangerous. It can be likened to travelling on an unknown journey without a road map.

Every business needs a strategy, which is the definition of the actions that must be to meet its objectives. A business strategy must embrace needs and concerns of all business units by avoiding conflicts as it seeks to achieve goals for sustain the business. The purpose of the business, its target market, strengths and product lines need to be clearly spelt out in the strategy.

An effective strategy must differentiate a business from its competitors in areas including price differentiation, unique product lines, customisation and niche marketing.

Michael Porter (1996) defines a business strategy as 'a distinctive value proposition and a different customised value chain with clear trade-offs coming together to ensure continuity of the business'.

The process of developing a strategy involves an analysis of the current status of the business; a strategic direction of where the business aims to be; desired objectives; a strategic team and regular reviews. A strategy map, soft systems methodology and a strategy road map can help to achieve a good business strategy.

Strategy Map

Strategy maps provide the tools needed for communicating the strategy of a business and the tools to help in the implementation of the strategy (Kaplan & Norton, 2000). Developed by Kaplan and Norton (2004), strategy maps have four distinct sections—financial, customer, internal processes, and learning and growth, which also correspond with the four perspectives of the balance scorecard.

Creation of a Strategy Map

To create a strategy map, the following steps must be followed:

1. There must be four perspectives, namely financial, customer, internal and learning and growth.
2. All information must be captured on one page to enable easy communication.
3. The processes must be supported by the allocation of human capital, information resources, leadership and teamwork.

4. Relationships between cause and effect are illustrated by connecting arrows.

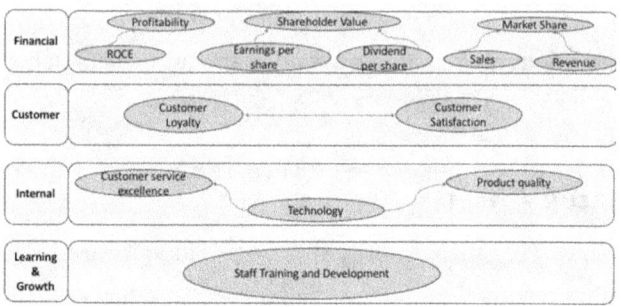

Benefits of Strategy Maps

By linking shareholder value creation, core capabilities, human resources, information technology and innovation, organisational design, learning, customer and process management with one another in a single graphical representation, strategy maps are a great resource in the description and communication of an organisation's strategy between the executive and to the other employees. This creates an alignment around the strategy for the successful implementation of the strategy as a result of the following:

1. It provides a simple and clean visual representation that can be easily referred to. A strategy map is visually attractive and easier to remember than a scribbled note or an email.

2. Different goals are merged into a single strategy. Floating ideas of a company's strategy are given conceptual home, in a strategy that easily be interpreted.

3. Every employee is given a clear goal for the attainment of Key Performance Indicators (KPIs). Therefore, knowledge of the strategy is not limited to members of the leadership team.
4. Elements of the strategy that need special attention can easily be identified since all the important goals are laid out in plain sight.

Soft Systems Methodology (SSM)

Soft systems methodology (SSM) is a method for handling problematic and chaotic situations. It is an action-oriented process of reviewing challenging situations where solutions are obtained by examining the situation and taking the needed actions for improvement (Checkland & Poulter, 2010).

SSM is primarily used in the analysis of complex situations with divergent views about the problem definition. Examples of these situations which are known as "soft problems" include issues such as the following: How to improve primary education and the best treatment for mentally ill criminal offenders.

The Soft Systems Methodology (SSM) was developed from a research conducted at Lancaster University, which applied systems engineering approaches to solve management and business problems. On realising that hard systems approach was not the best approach to fixing business problems, Peter Checkland, a Professor in systems engineering, put together a pragmatic and practical approach to identify and solve "soft" problems through action research. The soft systems methodology includes a set of tools which include CATWOE, rich picture and conceptual model (Burge, 2015).

Stages of Soft System Methodology

Checkland P. (1999) splits the soft system methodology into seven stages.

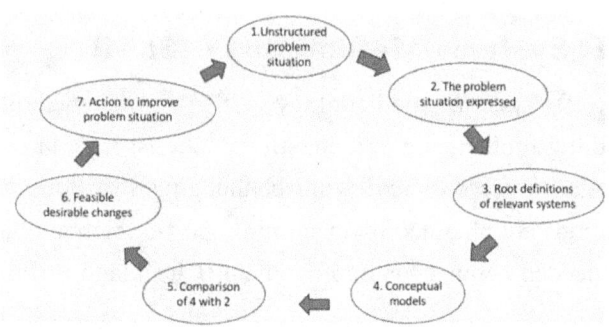

Stages 1: Problem Identification

This stage concerns the real world and information gathering about the problematic situation. An understanding of the problem is sought holistically. This can be done through interviews, observations and workshops.

It is imperative to view this stage as an introduction to expressing the problem situation or a means of moving to a state of understanding the problem situation.

Stage 2: Expression of Problem Situation

This stage involves the statement and justification of the problem situation. The explanation of the problem and its relationship with other issues is done using a "Rich Picture". The construction of a rich picture for a particular situation allows identification of differing interpretation and permits agreements on the interpretation of the problem.

Stage 3: Root Definitions

This is an important stage in the soft systems methodology because the root definition is a statement of purpose which captures the crux of the situation of the relevant system. Root definitions of relevant systems are developed in state three through the use of the CATWOE analysis. The CATWOE which is an acronym for customers, actors, transformation, worldview, owner and environment; aids the development of the root definition through the provision of the answers to "what has to be achieved", "how it has to be achieved" and the environmental restrictions which affect the course of transformation.

Stage 4: Conceptual Models

Stage four is where conceptual models are developed. This stage also subjects the Root Definition to the 5Es test of Efficacy, Effectiveness, Efficiency, Ethicality and Elegance.

Stage 5: Comparison of Conceptual Models with the Real World

In the fifth stage, different conceptual models are compared to the reality. This comparison is meant to initiate dialogue leading to the identification of changes for the improvement of the situation.

Stage 6: Definition of Desirable and Feasible Changes

The sixth stage assesses the feasibility and desirability of the proposed changes in the real world.

Stage 7: Taking Action for the Improvement of the Problem Situation

The application of the model is done in the last stage. Once the desirable and feasible changes have been identified, all efforts are channelled towards the implementation.

Benefits of SSM

Soft Systems Methodology aids with structuring complex organisational and political situations by allowing users to deal with the issues in an organised manner. It also compels other solutions apart from technical ones to be identified. The soft system methodology offers a more acceptable fit between people and systems and enables the resolution of unresolved problems or issues (Forbes, P. and Checkland, P.B., 1987). SSM also gives problems which are not well defined a better structure by classifying and focusing on the pertinent systems that allows them to be handled in an organised manner.

It is imperative to note that the SSM can be started with any activity, developed in any direction and substantial used at any stage because the methodology is flexible and can be custom-made to suit the needs of an organisation. The soft system methodology is an involving process, allowing the contribution of stakeholders in debating the issues to reach at a mutually agreed root definition. Gharahedaghi, J. and Kaufman, M. (2011).

The importance of the soft systems methodology cannot be overemphasised; however, it also has a few limitations. In the fourth stage of the system which deals with the development of conceptual models, neither a modelling tool nor technique exists for the comparison of solutions in the real world. There is also the need for factoring in the effectiveness of system thinking. Working with SSM requires a user who can adapt to novel approaches. Assembling the rich picture without a specified structure or solution for the problem situation can also prove a challenging task. Other critics of the soft system methodology assert that since the methodology is still in the development stage, its adoption by industry is still very low. Meadows, D. (2008).

CATWOE

CATWOE is a root definition agenda which enables a complete approach to be built for a system and its fundamentals from diverse viewpoints.

A little after a decade after Peter Checkland had developed the Soft Systems Methodology (SSM), in 1975, a researcher in the same department with Peter Checkland called David Smyth, observed that the SSM was more effective when considered in relation to the following elements: Customers/Clients, Actors, Transformation Process, World View, Owner, and Environmental Constrains. These elements collectively referred to by the acronym CATWOE. The CATWOE checklist is used to study a system by stressing a root definition, that outlines the system that encompasses the conversion of inputs into outputs. The various elements of the CATWOE analysis are listed in the table below.

C	Customers	Beneficiaries of the business process and how they are affected by the issues.
A	Actors	Those responsible for the implementation of the solution.
T	Transformation	The change resulting from the system or the process.
W	Worldview	The big picture and its wider impact.
O	Owner	Contribution of the owners of the situation to the solution process.
E	Environment	Environmental constraints impacting on the success of the solution.

Rich Picture

A Rich Pictures is a compilation of pictures, symbols, drawings, and text that represent a situation. They are a diagrammatic way of relating experiences and perceptions to a problem situation through the identification and linkage of a series of ideas. Rich pictures were designed as part of Checkland's Soft Systems Methodology (Checkland, 1999) for gathering data about complex situations by providing a means for learning about complex problems through detailed ("rich") pictorial representations. Some of the elements of a rich picture include a title, symbols, keywords, sketches, cartoons, arrows and other lines to showing relationships and flow of resources.

Strategy Roadmap

A strategy roadmap links a strategy to its execution by visualising the critical expected outcomes to specific time horizons for the achievement of the firm's strategic vision.

To ensure a clear bridge between a strategy and its roadmap, the transformation of a strategy to its roadmap must be done logically and in a structured manner which supports the strategic vision of the organisation.

The main components of a strategy roadmap define a desired destination by stating the goals; timelines for achieving the goals while considering any unforeseen hitches; practical stages necessary to get to the desired destination. It considers interdependencies among steps and anticipates alternative routes that help optimise resource allocation and minimise risks.

Process

Road mapping is a collaborative strategic planning process. The first stage is to determine a vision, which is a desirable future state that the business would like to have happen. Next, several vision statements are expressed and concrete goals are defined. The third stage is doing a gap analysis. Here, critical capabilities needed for the articulated visions are determined; then, a gap analysis between available capabilities and the needed capabilities is conducted. Finally, a portfolio of actions based on the gap analysis is recommended.

Application

A clothing retail company with a strong brand and wide international presence lacks proper customer segmentation. By trying to satisfy all customer segments the retailer has had part of its market share taken by competitors specialising in different customer segments.

The company therefore decided on a strategy of implementing the balanced scorecard to align the activities of the clothing section to the vision of making the retailer relevant, profitable and truly sustainable.

This proposed balanced scorecard will enable the retail company to clarify their vision and strategy and translate them into measurable actions. It will also provide feedback to ensure a continuous improvement in performance and results. When deployed completely, this balanced scorecard will change strategic planning from a theoretical exercise to being the pivot of the operations of the clothing retailer.

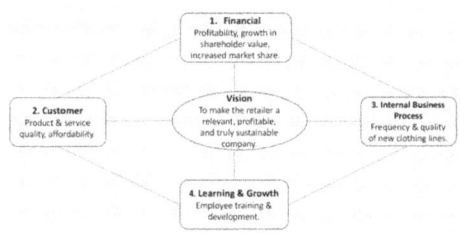

Road Map for the Implementation of the Balanced Scorecard

To ensure a successful introduction of the balanced scorecard, the retailer must follow the road map in the figure below, which involves the dissemination of the company's vision with key stakeholders to obtain consensus and a confirmation of focus and priorities. An implementation committee must then be set up to plan strategic interventions, integrate the Balance Score Card into the organisational strategy of the company, set targets for the implementation of the strategy and determine strategic actions to be taken. Finally, there must be a monitoring and evaluation system for reviewing the strategic outcomes.

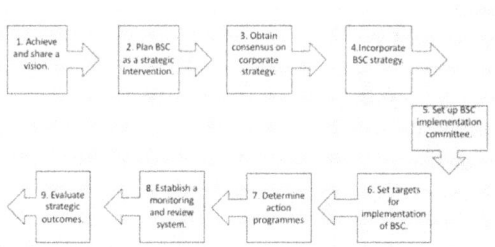

Conclusion

The journey to creating a successful business through effective business management practices has been highlighted. Success in today's highly competitive and global business environment requires professionals with the right acumen to steer the affairs towards profitability by creating and managing value through transformation, innovation, change, effective leadership and strategy.

The choice is yours to either keep an underperforming business or grab the opportunity of building a company where the value created is maintained and multiplied through good leadership for the transformation of the organisation, innovation and effective strategies.

I help my clients through these processes by providing bespoke and practical solutions to suit their business needs.

References

Appelbaum, S. H., Habashy, S., Malo, J.L. and Shafiq, H., 2012. Back to the future: revisiting Kotter's 1996 change model. *Journal of Management Development,* 31(8), pp. 764–782.

Awadallah, E. A. and Allam, A., 2015. A critique of the Balanced Scorecard as a Performance Management Tool. *International Journal of Business and Social Science,* 6(7), p. Online.

Birkmose, H., 2017. *Shareholders' Duties (European Company Law).* Alphen aan den Rijn: Kluwer Law International.

Cameron, E. and Green, M., 2009. *Making sense of Change Management.* 2nd ed. London: Kogan Page.

Casey, W. and Peck, W., 2004. *A Balanced View of Balanced Scorecard,* Denver: Executive Leadership Group.

Chatham House, 2017. Contentious Borders: The Middle East and North Africa. *International Affairs,* 4(93), pp. 771–787.

Checkland, P., 1999. *Systems Thinking, Systems Practice.* Chihester: John Wiley and Sons Ltd.

Checkland, P. and Poulter, J., 2010. Soft Systems Methodology. In: M. Reynolds and S. Holwell, eds. *Soft Approaches to Managing Change.* London: Springer, pp. 191–242.

Connors, R. and Smith, T., 2012. *Change the Culture, Change the Game: The Breakthrough Strategy for Energizing Your Organization and Creating Accountability for Results.* New York: s.n.

COSO, 2004. *Eterprise Risk management—Intergrated Framework,* New York: COSO.

Crouhy, M., Galai, D. and Mark, R., 2014. *The Essentials of Risk Management.* 2nd Edition ed. New York: McGraw Hill.

Cummings, T. G. and Huse, E. F., 1989. *Organizational Development and Change.* Eagan, Minnesota: West Publishing Company.

Damodaran, A., 2005. Value and Risk: Beyond Betas. *Financial Analyts Journal,* 61(No. 2), pp. 38–43.

Degraff, J. and Quinn, S., 2006. *Leading Innovation: How to Jump Start Your Organization's Growth Engine.* New York: McGraw Hill Professional.

EQFM, 1988. *EQFM Excellence Model,* Brussels: EQFM.

EQFM, 2013. *EQFM Model 2013.* [Online] Available at:
https://www.efqm.org/index.php/efqm-model-2013/
[Accessed 2 September 2019].

Ferrel, B. D., 2012. *Accouting, Finances, Business and Adam Smith.* Kindle ed. s.l.:B. David Ferrel.

Friedemann, A. J., 2016. *When the Trucks Stop Running: Energy and the Future of Transportation.* New York: Springer.

Frisch, R., 1950. Alfred Marshall's Theory of Value. *The Quarterly Journal of Economics,* 64(4), pp. 495–524.

Fullan, M., 2004. *Leading in a Culture of Change.* New Jersey: John Wiley and Sons.

Fries, K., 2018. *Forbes: 8 Essential Qualities That Define Great Leadership.* [Online] Available at:
https://www.forbes.com/sites/kimberlyfries/2018/02/08/8-essential-qualities-that-define-great-leadership/#7ad364e83b63 [Accessed 25 July 2019].

Goffin Keith and Mitchell Rick, 2005. *Innovation Framework: Startegies and Implementation Using the Pentathlon Framework.* 2nd ed. Ontario: Palgrave Macmillan.

Goffin, K. and Mitchell, R., 2016. *Innovation Management: Effective Strategy and Implementation.* 3 ed. London: Palgrave Publishing.

Goleman, D., 2000. Leadership that gets results. *Harvard Business Review,* Issue March–April, pp. 78–90.

Goodley, S. and Ashby, J., 2015. Revealed: How Sports Direct pays below the minimum wage. *The Guardian*, 9 December, p. Online.

Harry, M. and Schroeder, R., 2006. *Six Sigma: The Breakthrough Management Strategy Revolutionizing the World's Top Corporations.* Paperback ed. New York: Doubleday.

Hill, T. and Westbrook, R., 1997. SWOT ANALYSIS: it's time for a product recall. *Long Range Planning,* 30(1), pp. 46–52.

Hoogendoorn, S., 2013. The Impact of Gender Diversity on the Performance of Business Teams: Evidence from a Field Experiment. *Management Science,* 59(7), pp. 1514–1528.

House, R. J. et al., 2004. *Culture, Leadership and Organizations.* Thousand Oaks: Sage Publications.

International Organization for Standardization, 2018. *Risk,* Geneva: ISO.

J., L. and H., I., 2005. *The Johari Window, a graphical model of interpersonal awareness.,* Los Angeles: University of Carlifonia.

Kaplan, R. S. and Norton, D. P., 1992. The Balanced Scorecard—Measures that Drive Performance. *Harvard Business Review,* Issue January–February.

Kaplan, R. S. and Norton, D. P., 2000. *Having Trouble with Your Strategy? Then Map It.* [Online] Available at: https://hbr.org/2000/09/having-trouble-with-your-strategy-then-map-it
[Accessed 21 August 2019].

Kaplan, R. S. and Norton, D. P., 2002. *The Balanced Scorecard.* s.l.:Harvard Press Review.

Kaplan, R. S. and Norton, D. P., 2004. *Strategy Maps: Converting Intangible Assets into Tangible Outcomes.* Boston, Massachusetts: Harvard Business School Publishing.

Kotter, J. P., 2012. *Leading Change.* Brighton Massachusetts: Harvard Business Review Press.

Lam, J., 2017. *Implementing Enterprise Risk Management: From Methods to Applications.* Hoboken, New Jersey: John Wiley and Sons Inc.

London School of Commerce, 2017. *Interpersonal Leadership,* London: LSC Online Portal.

Madsen, D. O. and Stenheim, T., 2014. Perceived Benefits of Balanced Scorecard Implementation: Some Preliminary Evidence. *Problems and Perspectives in Management,* 12(3), pp. 81–90.

Mahajan, G., 2016. *Value Creation: The Definitive Guide for Business Leaders.* New Delhi: Sage.

McGuffog, T., 2016. *Building Effective Value Chains: Value and its Management.* London: Kogan Page Ltd.

Menon, A., Bharadwaj, S. G., Adidam, P. T. and Edison, S. W., 1999. Antecedents and Consequences of Marketing Strategy Making: A Model and a Test. *Journal of Marketing,* 63(2), pp. 18–40.

Miles, M. B. and Huberman, A. m., 2014. *Qualitative Data Analysis.* 3rd ed. Los Angeles: Sage publications.

Mitchell, R., 2011. *The Innovation Pentathlon,* Cranfield: Cranfield School of Management.

Monk, E. F. and Wagner, B. J., 2013. *Concepts in Enterprise Resource Planning.* 4th ed. Ohio: Mason.

Northouse, P. G., 2016. *Leadership: Theory and Practice.* 7th ed. Los Angeles: Sage Publications.

Pahl, N. and Richter, A., 2007. *SWOT Analysis—Idea, Methodology and A Practical Approach.* Munich: GRIN Verlag.

Parliamentary Business, 2016. *Mike Ashley must be accountable for Sports direct working practices.,* London: UK Parliament.

Pessanha, D. S. and Prochnik, V., 2006. *Practioners' Opinions on Academics' critics on the Balanced Scorecard,* Rio de Janeiro: Federal University of Rio de Janeiro.

Porter, M. E., 1980. *Competitive Strategy: Techniques for Analyzing Industries and Competitors.* New York: Free Press.

Porter, M. E., 1996. What is Strategy? *Harvard Business Review,* Volume Nov–Dec, pp. 1–19.

Porter, M. E., 2008. The Five Competitive Forces Tha Shape Strategy. *Harvard Business Review,* pp. 24–41.

Rezaee, Z., 2008. *Corporate Governance and Ethics.* London: John Wiley and Sons.

Robbins, S. P., 2003. *Organizational Behavior.* 10 ed. Texas: Prentice Hall Inc.

Robertson, H., 2015. *PESTLE Analysis for Business.* California: CreateSpace Independent Publishing Platorm.

Ross, J., 1999. *Total Quality Management: Text, Cases and Readings.* 3rd ed. Boca Raton, Florida: CRC Press.

Rost, J. C., 1993. Leadership Development in the New Millennium. *Journal of Leadership and Organizational Studies,* 1(1), pp. 91–110.

Rowe, W. G. and Gorman, D., 2005. Leader succession and organizational performance: integrating the common-sense,ritual scapegoating, and vicious-circle succession theories. *The Leadership Quarterly,* 16(2), pp. 197–219.

Schein, E. H., 1996. Culture: The Missing Concept in Organization Studies. *Administrative Science Quarterly,* 41(2), p. 62.

Shen, G. Q. and Yu, a. T., 2012. Value Management: Recent Developments and Way Forward. *Construction Innovation,* 12(3), pp. 264–271.

The Cadbury Committee, 1992. *The Financial Aspects of Corporate Governance,* London: Gee.

The Economic Times, 2018. *The Economic Times.* [Online] Available   at: https://economictimes.indiatimes.com/definition/shareholder -value
[Accessed 19 September 2018].

The Financial Reporting Council, 2018. *The UK Corporate Governance Code,* London: The Financial Reporting Council Ltd.

The Institute of Value Management, 2018. *The Institute of Value Management.* [Online] Available at: ivm.org.uk [Accessed 23 August 2018].

Tricker, B., 1998. *Pocket Director: Essentials of Corporate Governance.* 3rd ed. London: Profile Books.

Uhl, A. and Gollenia, L. A., 2012. *A Handbook of Business Transformation Management Methodology.* London: Routledge.

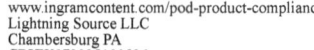